I will; persevere

Evelyn Copping

BookLeaf
Publishing

Presentation by *BookLeaf Publishing*

Web: www.bookleafpub.com

E-mail: info@bookleafpub.com

ISBN: 9789357617932

First edition 2023

This book is dedicated to everyone who has ever told me that I was a talented writer and should gather my poems into a book. Your words of encouragement have given me the strength to share my words in hopes they might resonate with someone else's journey. I thank you all for your inspiration.

Circle of Scars

It is a vicious circle of torment, sorrow, and
death
No one could have predicted the horror
Everyone shares in the suffering and
Feels the pain
They sit silent as they hope for
Their luck to change
They will always carry with them the scars
Of what has taken place here
Although the damage has already been done
In their heads they still hear
The screams of brutality

Written April 27, 1999

A firework

My love for him
Is like a firework
Beautiful at first
But destined to burn out

Written July 1, 2000

I am a Bumble Bee

3

I am a Bumble Bee
I will not question if I can fly or not
I have wings for a reason
I am a Bumble Bee
I will not doubt that my wings are not strong
enough
For they were given to me so that I could soar

Written Summer 2011

How it feels

C-PTSD robs you of your happy days
The days when you should be filled with joy
A scent, a noise, or a word comes along
And you get thrown back into the middle of a
memory
So intense you believe you are there
Standing in front of that monster again

Fiery breath kissing your cheek
Frozen against the urge to run
Then in a flash, it is over
You come back to reality
Mind racing, heart pounding, and
Gasping to catch your breath

As people stare and your anxiety flares
You try calming yourself
Some days everything clicks, and you feel better
Other times your anxiety wins and
You spiral further down the rabbit hole

Getting tangled up like you are walking through a
spider web
Say what you will
C-PTSD feels this way to me

Written August 11, 2015

Even if I'm happy

Even if I'm happy
Blue skies turn to grey
Raindrops fall upon my head
Darkness finds its way in

Even if I'm happy
I can see it all about to end
The waves that will come crashing in
And knock me down again

Even if I'm happy
In this moment that we are in
I can't help but fear the other side
That pain that was my friend

Even if I'm happy
Today is not the end
Another day is approaching soon
I might be weaker then

Even if I'm happy I feel it's just a dream
That soon I will awaken
To see the monster that is me

Even if I'm happy

This world seems not for me
Like I have done so wrong before
The torment must be fed

Written December 10, 2015

First Day

Nervous
Glad, excited
Sweaty palms, bubbly smile
Ready to take on this challenge
Prepared

Written August 23, 2016

Change

Summer turns to autumn
Green changes to yellow
Hot fades to cool
Clothes grow longer
Days become shorter
Time eternally changing
One thing to the next

Written August 25, 2016

Stress?

Headache
Pain
Pounding, Throbbing, Squeezing
Pressure
Agony

Written May 16, 2017

Grey sky

Cloudy, Dark
      Rain against the window
Pitter, patter
      Patter, pitter
Heart is crying

Is love real?
      Drops grow bigger
Splitter, splatter
      Now I'm drowning

Written May 16, 2017

Days

On my good days
I want to dance every second of the day
Songs run through my head
And my body can't help but move along

On my bad days
It takes everything I have inside me
Just to leave the bed
Flashes of heartache playing in my mind

But then I'm on top of the world
Singing like life is a musical

Then in what seems like a second
I envision myself stepping off the curb
Just as a bus goes by
Throwing my body skidding across the
pavement

Written May 26, 2017

I apologize

I apologize

for the way my mind works
for getting upset at situations only real in my
head

I apologize

for making you pay for their mistakes
for not being able to differentiate between truth
and fiction

I apologize

for giving my heart in pieces
for not knowing how to love properly

Written October 30, 2018

Depression

Dark thoughts run through my head
Erasing all the constructive work I've done
Positive my end is near
Reminiscence of better days isn't for me
Expressing my feelings just shouldn't be done
Sabotage is my new favorite pastime
Shamefully I sit in silence
Imagining my own death
Obsessing over things I can't control
Numb to the pain that embraces me

Written June 18, 2020

Society has changed

Hellos were met with
Warm smiles and tight hugs

> Now we must wave from a distance
> And just blow a kiss

Shopping was something that was
Done just to pass the time

> Has turned into more of a battlefield
> Everyone rushing to buy supplies
> Before stores run out

Going out to restaurants,
Movies, clubs and friend's houses
Was overrated

> Now it is longed for by many
> Even some introverts

A cough or a sneeze once
Met with 'bless you'

> Has turned into dirty looks, glares,
> And judgement of 'they must have it'

Innocent until proven guilty
No longer seems true

                    Society has changed
          Welcome to the normal new

Written June 19, 2020

Never to return

Trapped in the past unable to move forward
I beg for death to pull me under
So that my guilt will be set free
But that is not the way this goes

Yesterday I thought I was fine
But now something is bugging me
What it is, I do not know
But feel it deep inside of me

This turning of tides as waves crash
Washing over me
Eroding what I used to be
Is there anything left of me

I wonder as my thoughts fade
Would anyone miss me
If I were gone for good
Never to return again

Or would the memory of me
Fade with time
Like a warm summer breeze
Into the fall night

Written March 9, 2021

Today

Today I sat and thought of you
Of the times we have shared
And the moments you'll never get to see

Today I cried for you
For the time taken from you way too soon
And the heartache left behind

Today I heard a joke you would have loved
I went to call you to share it with you
Then I remembered you are gone

Today I cried for all the guilt
I have over words left unsaid
And moments not shared

Today I said goodbye to your ashes
Like I really wish I'd said to your face
Life is funny that way

Written April 6, 2021

Drowning

I feel like I am drowning
Like the waves are crashing into me
Knocking me back
Pushing me under
And just as I reach the surface
As I am gasping for air
I see a boat on the horizon
So close I am sure they would hear
If I just called out for help
But I'm frozen in fear
Of what they might think

Then another wave crashes against me
Knocking me under once more
When I reach the surface again
The waters are calm
The boat is retreating
The danger now gone
Why bother to sound the alarm?
They will only think you're a fake
How could anyone believe
You were actually drowning
With that life jacket around your neck

Written Summer 2022

Suicidal

Mixed emotions stirring in my head
Strange thoughts keep surfacing in my mind
Thoughts that scare me more than I'd like to
admit

Just put one foot forward, step off that curbside
Then everything will stop
Can it really be that simple?

But the moment has passed
And with it the danger

Later that evening doing the dishes
I pick up the sharp knife
And hold it for a minute

Suddenly I can feel the blood in my veins
The hard metal in my hand
Yearning to slide fiercely across my skin

A voice breaks through
I'm back in the kitchen

Next morning I wake
With this lump in my throat

This intense feeling of tension

Just begging for my thumb
To press hard against it
Until I gasp for air

I know in that moment
I don't want to die

I don't want to suffer, feel useless or weak
Don't want to be vulnerable again
To have my words and feelings used against me

I fight back the urge to cry
And wonder will I make it another year
Another month, week or day

Time holds these answers
But refuses to share them with me

Written October 7, 2022

A smile, then a glance

A smile, then a glance
I look away quickly
Not sure if I should take a chance
And tell you how hot you are

I hold it in from you but tell our friend
How I like your smile, and the passion when you
speak
How wonderful it would be to be your girlfriend
She says that you like my smile

I'm as giddy as a schoolgirl
At the thought of you liking me
You make me want to dance and twirl
Telling the world I'm happy

Every time I see that you are online
I wave, but nothing more
Just hoping you'll notice and give me a sign
Letting know you actually want to be with me

And then it happens that wonderful day
You say hello back and the conversation starts
We talk for a few weeks before I say
Would you like to hang out?

A few hangouts together with my children
Before we finally go out solo
We walked and talked until I was frozen
It was a night to remember; that I wanted to last
forever

Written October 11, 2022

Future

Forever wondering what comes next
Uncovering my past to understand the future
Thinking and rethinking everything I've done
Until I don't know what's right or true
Regretting what I've said in frustration
Eternally worried about what my fate holds

Written October 12, 2022

Persevere

Persisting thoughts of my own demise
embody my soul making me
relish in depictions only a depressed mind can understand
scared I will not make it
eager to prove that I will
visualizing my future as bright as can be
eventually my mood improves a little
right before I crash again
eroding all the changes I had made

Written: October 20, 2022